SCIENCE STARTERS

Water Play

Wendy Madgwick

RSVP

RAINTREE
STECK-VAUGHN
P U B L I S H E R S
The Steck-Vaughn Company

Austin, Texas

Titles in this series:
Up in the Air • Water Play • Magnets and Sparks
Super Sound • Super Materials • Light and Dark
Living Things • On the Move

© Copyright 1999, text, Steck-Vaughn Company

Published by Raintree Steck-Vaughn Publishers, an imprint of Steck-Vaughn Company

Words that appear in **bold** in the text are explained in the glossary on page 30.

Illustrations: Catherine Ward/ Simon Girling Associates
Photographer: Andrew Sydenham
Picture Acknowledgments:
pages 5, 6, 13 left, 13 right Zefa; page 15 FLPA/ H. Eisenbeiss.

Library of Congress Cataloging-in-Publication Data
Madgwick, Wendy.
Water play / Wendy Madgwick.
    p.   cm.—(Science Starters)
Includes bibliographical references and index.
Summary: Provides instructions for a variety of projects that demonstrate the properties and uses of water.
ISBN 0-8172-5326-2
1. Water—Juvenile literature.
[1. Water—Experiments. 2. Experiments.]
I. Title. II. Series: Madgwick, Wendy, Science starters.
GB662.3.M33   1998
532—dc21   98-40752

Printed in Italy. Bound in the United States.
1 2 3 4 5 6 7 8 9 0 03 02 01 00 99

Contents

Looking at Water

This book has lots of fun activities to help you find out about water. Here are some simple rules you should follow before doing an activity.

- Always tell an adult what you are doing. Ask him or her if you can do the activity.
- Read through the activity before you begin. Collect all the materials you will need and put them on a tray. They are listed on page 28.
- Make sure you have enough space to set up your activity.
- Follow the steps carefully. Ask an adult to help you cut things.
- Watch what happens carefully. Some things happen quickly, but other things take a long time.
- Keep a notebook. Draw pictures or write down what you did and what happened.
- Always clear up when you have finished. Wash your hands.

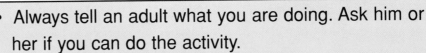

▶ Water flows downhill. When a river flows over the edge of a cliff to a lower level, it forms a waterfall.

Wet Water

There is more water than dry land on Earth. This water falls from the sky as rain, snow, or hail. It collects in rivers and lakes. Water flows downhill until it reaches the sea.

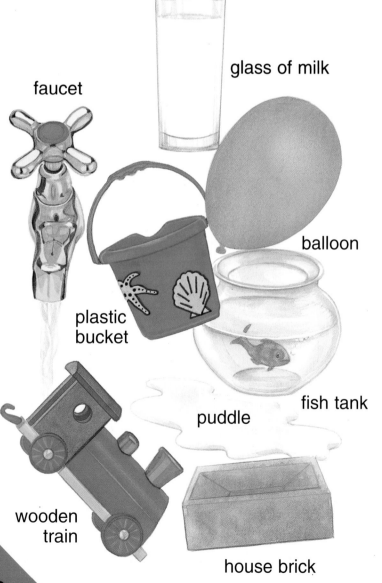

faucet

glass of milk

balloon

plastic bucket

fish tank

puddle

wooden train

house brick

When the sun comes out some of the snow **melts**. It turns to water.

◀ Wet and dry

Is water wet or dry?
In this picture four things are wet and four are dry. Make a list of, or draw, some more things that are wet.

Note: The materials you will need for this project and all the activities in this book are listed on Page 28.

6

Catching rain

How much rain falls where you live?
You can find out.

1 Ask an adult to cut the top off a plastic bottle.

2 Use a ruler to mark a scale on a piece of paper. Tape the paper to the outside of the bottle.

3 Put the top into the bottle as shown.

4 Put your rain measure outside. Make sure it is not sheltered from the rain.

5 Each week look to see how much rain is in the bottle.
Don't forget to empty it each week.

Stay or Go?

Water is a liquid. It can flow and spread out. It can also soak into things. Let's find out what shapes it can make.

Level lines

1 Pour some water into a bottle. Stand the bottle on a table. Look at the water surface. It is level with the table.

2 Tilt the bottle to one side. Is the water surface still level with the table? Look at the picture to see what happens.

Pour water into a cup or on to the ground outside. See what happens to the water. Describe the shape the water makes each time. Liquids usually take the shape of their containers.

Soak it up

1 Pour some water into a saucer. What happens to it? The water takes the shape of the saucer. The saucer does not soak up the water.

3 Put the sponge on a plate. Gently pour water on to the sponge. What happens to the water? It soaks into the sponge. What happens to the sponge? It feels wet.

2 Now take a dry sponge and squeeze it. Does it feel soft or hard?

4 Squeeze the sponge over a bowl. Water comes out. The sponge has soaked up the water. When you squeeze the sponge, you force out the water.

All Gone

Rain makes puddles, but they do not last for long. When the sun shines, the water dries up. We say the water has **evaporated**. Where does the water go?

Quick drying

1 Wet four sheets of paper towel.

▲ Why do we hang out washing to dry? Where do clothes dry best? You will find the answer in this experiment.

2 Lay one piece of the wet paper towel in the sun and one in the shade. Hang another on a washing line. Squeeze one into a ball. Check them every five minutes. Which one dries first?

Drying out

1 Pour the same amount of water into two glasses. Mark the water levels with a felt-tipped pen. Cover one glass with plastic wrap.

2 Put the glasses in a warm place. Look at them after a few days. Which glass has less water in it?
The uncovered glass has less water. The sun warmed the water. The water turned into droplets called **water vapor**, which went into the air.

Look at the covered glass. Can you see water drops on the underside of the plastic wrap? The water vapor could not escape. It turned back to water on the cool plastic wrap.

Liquid or Solid?

Water can be a liquid, solid ice, or a **gas** called water vapor. Water vapor is made up of tiny drops of water. You cannot see it, but you can turn it back into water.

Magic water

You can make water appear out of thin air.

1 Pour some cold water into a glass. Put it in the refrigerator for a few hours.

2 Take the glass out and leave it in a warm room. Can you see water droplets on the side of the glass? The water drops have come from water vapor in the air. This vapor cools down on the cold glass. As it cools it forms drops of water. This is called **condensation**.

◄ Look at this photo. The water on the stems is called **dew**. Where did it come from? (Think about the water on the cold glass on page 12.)

These twigs are covered with ▶ **frost**. The dew freezes on the twigs to form frost.

Freeze it

Fill a small bottle with a narrow neck with water. Do not put the lid on. Put the bottle in a freezer. Leave it until the water has frozen.

Where is the top of the ice? Is it above or below the top of the bottle? Ice takes up more space than water, so the ice will be above the top.

13

A Magic Skin

The top, or surface, of water is special. Drops of water cling together tightly. They make a see-through "skin." This is called **surface tension**. Let's find out how we can tell this skin is there.

Water walker ▶
This is a water strider. It can walk on water. See the dents its feet make in the water's skin.

Surface view

1 Fill a tall glass to the top with water.

2 Bend down so that your eyes are level with the top of the water.

What shape is the water surface? It should curve downward in the center.

3 Drop in a few dried peas or tiny stones. Does the water overflow?

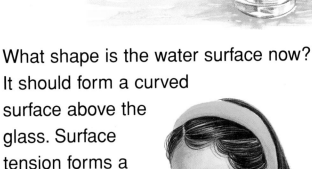

What shape is the water surface now? It should form a curved surface above the glass. Surface tension forms a "skin" that holds the water in the glass.

14

A solid surface

1. Fill a bowl with water.

2 Cut a small piece of thick plastic. Carefully put the plastic on top of the water. What happens? The plastic floats on the water.

3 Tear off a small piece of paper towel. Put a metal pin on top of it. Float the paper and pin on the water.

See what happens to the pin and the paper. The paper will sink, leaving the pin floating on the surface.

Bubble Power

We can change the surface skin of water. We can even make it stretch. This "stretchy" skin lets us have some fun. We can blow bubbles. All we need is some detergent.

Bright bubbles

Look at this picture of bubbles.
What is inside a bubble?

What is around the outside of the bubble?

A bubble is a ball of air enclosed in a stretchy, liquid skin.

Mixing bubbles

1 To make bubble mix, half-fill a mug with warm water.

2 Add about three teaspoonfuls of detergent. Mix well.

Blowing bubbles

You can make a bubble blower from a piece of plastic-covered wire.

1 Bend one end of the wire into a circle. Leave some wire at the end of the circle. Twist the two ends together to make the handle.

2 Dip your bubble blower into the mix. Blow gently. What shape are the bubbles?

Are bubbles always the same shape? Make a square blower. What shape are the bubbles? Now try other shapes. What did you find out about the shape of bubbles?
Bubbles are always round.

Going Up!

Water usually flows downhill. But it can also go upward. Water flows up plant stems.

Tiny tubes

Put a small stick of celery into some red-colored water.
Leave it for a few hours.
Cut the end off the celery. Look at it. Can you see the tubes that carry the water up the stem?
They should be colored red.

Fancy flowers

You will need some pale-colored flowers. White carnations work well. You also need some red and blue food coloring.

1 Cut off the bottom of the flower stem. Carefully cut up the middle of the stem.

2 Half-fill two glasses with water. Add a few drops of red coloring to one glass. Add blue coloring to the other glass.

3 Put one half of the flower stem into the blue water. Put the other half into the red water.

4 Leave the flower in a warm room for a few hours. What happens to it? Can you see that some petals have red streaks and others have blue streaks? The flower took up the colored water through its stem.

These flowers have blue, green, and red colored petals.

Papercraft

Paper is made up of lots of **fibers**. In between the fibers are tiny holes like tubes. Water will slowly rise up the paper through these holes.

Water lily

1 Cut several flower shapes from non-shiny colored paper. Fold the petals into the middle.

2 Put some of the flowers in a bowl of water. What happens to the petals? The petals will open as the paper **absorbs** the water.

Multi colors

We can use water movement through paper to find out what colors make up orange.

Then repeat steps 1 to 3, using a green pen or a purple pen.

1 Cut a long, thin strip of blotting paper. With an orange felt-tipped pen, color a thick band near one end. Tape the other end to a pencil.

Purple is made up of red and blue.

Orange is made up of red and yellow.

Green is made up of yellow and blue.

2 Ask an adult to cut the top off a small plastic bottle. Put a little water in the bottle. Balance the pencil across the top so that the end of the paper strip is in the water. The orange band must not touch the water. Leave for an hour.

3 Take the paper out of the water and let it dry. The color has moved up the paper. The orange band has separated into red and yellow.

Let's Mix It

Some solids seem to disappear when you stir them into water. We say they **dissolve**. Some liquids mix with water but others do not.

Mixing liquids

1 Half-fill a glass with water. Add some orange drink. What happens? The water and orange drink mix.

2 Put some water in a jar. Add cooking oil. Put on the lid and shake. Let the jar stand. What happens? The oil and water do not mix. The oil floats to the top.

◄ We use detergent to clean greasy dishes. The soapy water breaks up the grease into tiny drops. These float off the dishes and hang in the water, making it look cloudy.

Dissolve or not?

1 Pour some cold water into a glass. Mark the water level with a felt-tipped pen. Stir a spoonful of sugar into the water. It will dissolve. When things dissolve they do not take up more space. The water will stay at the same level.

2 Add another spoonful of sugar and stir again. Does the sugar disappear this time? Keep adding sugar. How many spoonfuls can you add before sugar stays at the bottom?

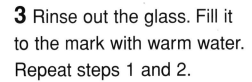

3 Rinse out the glass. Fill it to the mark with warm water. Repeat steps 1 and 2. How many spoonfuls of sugar can you add before some stays at the bottom? More sugar will dissolve in warm water.

Water Support

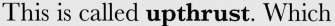

Some objects **sink** and others **float** in water. When an object is put into water, it pushes down on the water. The water pushes back. This is called **upthrust**. Which things float and which sink?

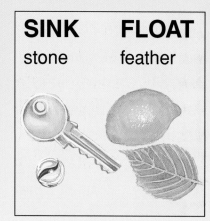

SINK	FLOAT
stone	feather

Put some objects in a bowl of water, one at a time. Make a list, or draw pictures, to show which objects float and which sink.

24

Sink it!

Can you make a sinker float?
Can you make a floater sink?
Let's try.

1 Half-fill a bowl with water. Fill a small plastic box with water and put its lid on. Put the box into the bowl. Does the box float or sink?

2 Take the box out of the bowl. Tip the water out of the box. Put the lid back on. Does the box float?

3 Take the lid off the box. Does the box still float?

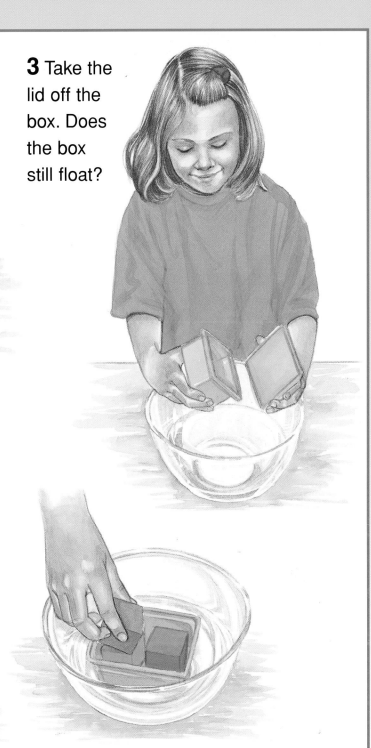

4 Put some toy bricks in the box. What happens to the box? How many bricks can you add before the box sinks?

An object sinks when the upthrust of the water is not strong enough to support it.

Floating Color

Liquids can also float and sink. It depends on their **density**. Dense liquids are heavy. They will sink in a less dense liquid.

Liquid sandwich

1 Pour some syrup into a tall glass. Gently pour on some oil. Does the oil float or sink? It will float.

2 Add some green coloring to cold water. Slowly pour it into the glass. Does it float or sink? The water will settle between the oil and the syrup.

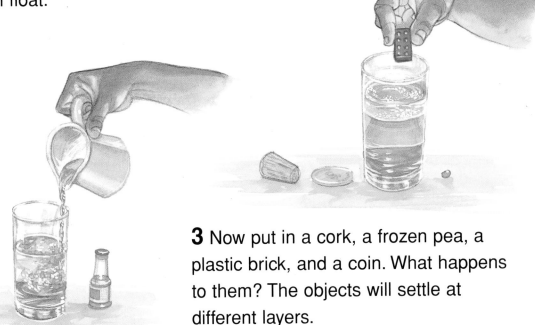

3 Now put in a cork, a frozen pea, a plastic brick, and a coin. What happens to them? The objects will settle at different layers.

Marbling

We can use floating oil paints to make colored paper. You can make your own.

Handy hint: If the oil paint is very thick, it may sink. Try using warm water in the bowl.

1 To make oil paints, put red powder paint into a clean plastic container. Add a little cooking oil and mix. Make blue oil paint in the same way.

4 Gently lay a piece of thick paper on to the water surface. Lift it off again at once. Let it drip into the bowl. Let your marbled paper dry.

2 Half-fill a large plastic bowl with water. Put it on newspaper.

3 Put a few drops of red and blue paint on to the water. Mix them with a stick.

27

Materials You Will Need

p. 6 *Wet Water*—paper, pencil, empty plastic bottle, ruler, tape, round-ended scissors.

p. 8 *Stay or Go?*—empty plastic bottle, cup, water, jug, saucer, plate, sponge, bowl.

p. 10 *All Gone*—large bowl, water, paper towel, washing line, clothespins, two drinking glasses, washable felt-tipped pen, plastic wrap.

p. 12 *Liquid or Solid?*—drinking glass, water, pitcher, small bottle with a narrow neck. You will need to put something in the refrigerator and something in the freezer.

p. 14 *A Magic Skin*—tall drinking glass, water, pitcher, dried peas or tiny stones, bowl, round-ended scissors, thick plastic, paper towel, metal pin.

p. 16 *Bubble Power*—mug, warm water, teaspoon, detergent, plastic-covered wire.

p. 18 *Going Up!*—small stick of celery, red and blue food coloring, fresh pale-colored flowers, water, three drinking glasses, round-ended scissors.

p. 20 *Papercraft*—non-shiny colored paper, round-ended scissors, large bowl, blotting paper, washable felt-tipped pens, tape, pencil, empty plastic bottle, water.

p. 22 *Let's Mix It*—two drinking glasses, orange drink, jar with a lid, cooking oil, teaspoon, sugar, cold and warm water.

p. 24 *Water Support*—bowl, water, small plastic box with a lid, toy wooden bricks, small objects to put in water.

p. 26 *Floating Color*—tall drinking glass, syrup, cooking oil, water, green food coloring, jug, cork, frozen pea, plastic brick, coin, colored oil paints or red and blue powder paint, clean plastic container, stick, large plastic bowl, newspaper, thick paper.

Hints to Helpers

Pages 6 and 7

Discuss how water flows downhill. Gravity and the contour of the land will determine the speed at which water flows downhill. All water on Earth settles at the lowest level it can reach.

Discuss the best place to put the rain measure. Keep it out of the wind. Push the measure firmly in the ground. Suggest that student keep a chart of how much rain falls each week.

Pages 8 and 9

Discuss the fact that the surface of liquids in containers always stays horizontal even when the container is tipped.

Water will soak into some things and not others. Try pouring water on different fabrics. Pour water on chalk, sand, and soil. Discuss how some rocks soak up water while others do not. Link this with the picture of the mountains and lake on page 6.

Pages 10 and 11

Water evaporates most quickly in a warm sunny place. Wind carries away the water vapor that evaporates from the surface of the cloth. This helps the cloth dry. Spreading out the cloth also helps the cloth dry, as water can evaporate from the whole surface. So the best drying conditions are warm, windy weather with the clothes spread out.

The heat from the sun makes the water in both glasses evaporate. But the plastic wrap stops the water vapor from escaping into the air. The water vapor condenses on the plastic wrap. Water drips back into the glass so that the level of the water stays higher in the covered glass. Discuss the water cycle and how evaporation and condensation work in nature.

Pages 12 and 13

The cold glass cools the air around it. Cool air cannot hold as much water as warm air, so some of the water vapor in the air condenses on the sides of the glass. Discuss where else you can see condensation, e.g., on the inside of windows on cold days or on a mirror in a steamy bathroom.

At night the air gets cooler and can hold less water vapor. The water vapor condenses on the cold surface of things such as plants. In the winter, the condensed water freezes and the ice particles form frost.

When water freezes it expands. Ice takes up more space than water. Discuss why water pipes sometimes burst in winter.

Page 15

The paper towel will absorb water and should sink. If it doesn't, you can gently push the wet paper down at one corner. The pin is left floating on the surface film. If you look carefully, you can see the "skin" bending beneath the pin.

Page 17

A better bubble mixture can be made by adding a few drops of glycerine.

Bubbles are always round because surface tension pulls the surface of the liquid into the smallest area. For a drop of water, the smallest possible area is a sphere.

Pages 18 and 19

Water travels up the flower through very narrow tubes in its stem by capillary action. These tubes should be seen clearly in the celery stem. The pull of this capillary action is enough to overcome the downward pull of gravity. In plants, the loss of water from the surface of petals and leaves (transpiration) also helps pull the water up the tubes.

Pages 20 and 21

The paper flowers open because the paper absorbs water. As the water rises through the paper fibers the paper swells up and the petals open.

The felt-tipped pens must be water soluble. The dyes in the pens dissolve in the water. The dissolved dyes move up the paper at different speeds. The different colors in the mixture separate as the water rises through the paper by capillarity.

Page 23

A certain volume of liquid can only dissolve a certain amount of solid. When no more solid will dissolve, a saturated solution is formed. The amount of solid that can dissolve depends on the temperature of the liquid. Warm liquids dissolve more solid than cold liquids.

Try a further test to see which things dissolve and which don't. Try peas and rice. The peas and rice do not dissolve.

Pages 24 and 25

Objects that are heavy for their size will sink. Those that are light for their size will float. You can show this very easily. Put a large ball of modeling clay into water. It will sink because it is dense and the upthrust of the water cannot support it. Now flatten the modeling clay into a boat shape with a large surface area. The boat will float. Try other shapes to see which float.

The box full of water may float low in the water or it may sink. If the amount of water displaced by the box weighs more than the box, the box will float. If the displaced water weighs less than the box, the box will sink. The empty box will float higher in the water than the box full of water. As bricks are added the upthrust of the water cannot support the box and it sinks.

Pages 26 and 27

The oil is the least dense liquid and will float on the water. The water is more dense than the oil but less dense than the syrup, so it floats on the syrup.

The objects also have different densities. The coin is very dense and will sink to the bottom. The cork has a low density and will float on the oil. The plastic brick will probably sink in the oil and float on the water, and a large frozen pea will sink in the water and float on the syrup. If the frozen pea is very small, its large surface area relative to its size may cause it to float on the water.

Much better results are achieved with household oil paints. Made-up oil paints must be very well mixed. The oil paints float on the water so you can lift them off with the paper. You can clean the water by placing a paper towel on the surface.

Glossary

Absorbs Soaks up liquids such as water.

Capillarity The rise of liquids such as water up a thin tube. Surface tension pulls the surface of a liquid up into narrow tubes.

Condensation The tiny drops of water that form on cold things. Water vapor cools down when it touches something cold. It turns into tiny water droplets that join to form larger drops.

Density The amount of weight an object has for its size.

Dew Water drops that form when water vapor in the air cools on cold surfaces. Dew often forms on plants at night.

Dissolve When some things are added to a liquid and mix completely with the liquid so they cannot be seen.

Evaporated Changed from a liquid or solid into a vapor or gas. Water changes into water vapor, which rises into the air.

Fibers Long, fine threads.

Float To stay on the surface of water or another liquid.

Frost The ice that forms on objects out of doors at night. Frozen dew.

Gas A substance that has no fixed shape. The tiny bits that make up a gas are spaced so far apart that they are not held together.

Melts When something changes from a solid into a liquid. When you warm ice, it melts into water. Some metals melt when you heat them.

Surface tension The stretchy "skin" on the surface of a liquid such as water. This skin is caused by the tiny drops of liquid clinging together very tightly at the surface.

Upthrust An upward push.

Sink To drop down into water or another liquid.

Water vapor Very tiny droplets of water in the air. They are too small for you to see but can condense on the surface of a cold object.

Further reading

Broekel, Ray. *Experiments with Water* (New True). Danbury, CT: Children's Press, 1988.

Challoner, Jack. *Floating and Sinking* (Start-Up Science). Austin, TX: Raintree Steck-Vaughn, 1996.

Gordon, Maria. *Float and Sink* (Simple Science). Austin, TX: Thomson Learning, 1995.

Wick, Walter. *A Drop of Water: A Book of Science and Wonder*. New York: Scholastic, 1997.

Wheeler, Jill. *Every Drop Counts: A Book About Water* (Target Earth). Edina, MN: Abdo and Daughters, 1993.

Index